~Emma's~ ESCAPE

A STORY OF AMERICA'S UNDERGROUND RAILROAD

by Sharon Shavers Gayle

Illustrated by Eric Velasquez

Little® Soundprints

To my mother, Mamie, who not only taught me to read, but also taught me that reading was the greatest shelter of all — S.S.G.

To the memory of all the courageous souls who freed themselves from slavery — E.V.

Published by Soundprints Division of Trudy Corporation, Norwalk, Connecticut.

Book design: Marcin D. Pilchowski
Editor: Laura Gates Galvin
Editorial assistance: Chelsea Shriver

First Edition 2003
10 9 8 7 6 5 4 3 2 1
Printed in China

Acknowledgments:
Our thanks to Joanna Banks of the Smithsonian Institution's Anacostia Museum and Center for African American History and Culture for her curatorial review.
Soundprints would also like to thank Ellen Nanney and Robyn Bissette at the Smithsonian Institution's Office of Product Development and Licensing for their help in the creation of this book.

Library of Congress Cataloging-in-Publication Data is on file with the publisher and the Library of Congress.

Table of Contents

A note to the reader:
Throughout this story you will see words in **bold letters**.
There is more information about these words in the
glossary. The glossary is in the back of the book.

Chapter 1
What's Wrong?

"Where's Emma?" asks Tomas. Tomas, Kevin, Emma and Lucy leave the Smithsonian Institution's Anacostia Museum and Center for African American History and Culture. The four best friends have been looking at an exhibit about African American life in the South before the Civil War. Emma follows behind slowly.

"I'm coming," Emma answers quietly.

"What's wrong?" Lucy asks.

"Slavery was so awful!" cries Emma.

"I know," agrees Kevin. "It was lucky that people were able to escape on the **Underground Railroad**."

"Let's go on the nature trail," says Tomas. Emma follows slowly behind her friends along the George Washington Carver Nature Trail.

"Tulips! Those are some of Mom's favorite flowers!" Emma says to herself. "Maybe I'll draw them for her." Emma pulls out some paper and begins to sketch.

"Emma!" a voice calls in a frantic whisper. "Where are you, Emma?"

"I'm right here," says Emma, as she gets up and turns around. She is surprised to see it's almost dark out. A thin girl who looks just a little older than Emma is standing in front of her.

The thin girl hugs Emma.

"Oh, Emma! Where were you? I'm so glad you're safe! We must go this minute. There may never be another chance to join your mother in Canada. We have to run!"

Suddenly, they hear the sound of barking dogs coming from the woods.

"Get down, Emma!" the girl whispers sharply.

Emma quickly drops to her hands and knees. She notices that she is no longer wearing shorts. She has on a dress made of rough material.

"Master Herrot set the dogs after us!" the girl whispers to Emma. "Your papa has a wagon waiting. We have to outrun those dogs!"

Chapter 2
Run for Freedom!

Emma and the girl scramble over rocks and twigs as the barking dogs get closer and closer.

"There's the wagon. Stay close," the girl whispers.

It is now completely dark. Emma feels strong hands grab her small ones and pull her into the air. Other hands push from behind. Suddenly, Emma finds herself inside the wooden wagon.

"Are you all right, Sister-Ann?" a deep voice asks.

"Yes, Ben-John. I'm fine," the girl says. "And Emma is all right, too."

"Emma, honey, get down low in the wagon," calls another man's voice. "You don't want to be seen."

Emma lies flat on her back. Two very small children snuggle next to her. The wagon begins to roll.

After hours of bumping along, the wagon stops.

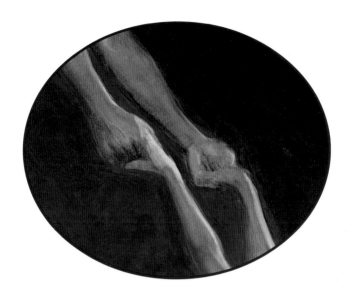

"All right, my girl," says Papa Roland, as his strong hands lift Emma out of the wagon. He carries her and begins to walk very fast.

Emma doesn't know where they are going or what they are doing. She is very frightened.

"Where are we?" Emma whispers to the man.

"We've just crossed from Georgia into South Carolina. We have to look for the man who is going to hide us," says Papa Roland. "The man is a **conductor** on the Underground Railroad."

"We're escaping!" Emma gasps. She remembers reading about the Underground Railroad, a system of people and places that helped slaves escape to freedom.

Ben-John and Sister-Ann follow behind Papa Roland and Emma. Each carries a small child. They are half-walking, half-running.

"Over here! Hurry, it's almost daylight!" a voice calls from the dark.

Chapter 3

The Journey Begins

An old man in a nightshirt stands in front of them. He is holding a lantern beside a well. Emma climbs down an old ladder deep into the empty well.

"Here are bread, cheese and fruit," says the man. He hands a sack down and then lowers a small pail of water. Emma hears the old man pull the ladder up and drag it away. Then he pulls the cover halfway across the top of the well.

A rooster crows and for a long time, nobody speaks.

"How did that man know we were coming?" Emma asks.

"He's part of the Underground Railroad. So is his niece. They arranged for us to hide in the wagon and this well. Now we will find your mama!" Papa Roland adds. He gives Emma's shoulder a loving squeeze. "I am so proud of your mama. It's hard to believe she escaped to the North all on her own!"

By now, Emma has figured out that Ben-John is Papa Roland's brother. She also knows that Sister-Ann is Ben-John's wife. They have four-year-old twins named Hester and DeVane. The twins hid with Emma in the wagon.

As the sun gets higher, it becomes stuffy in the dry, old well. Emma is too hot and sleepy to stand, so she slides to the ground. The men are too big to sit on the well floor. They move their feet to make room for Emma and the twins.

Chapter 4

A Close Call

From above, Emma thinks she hears thunder, but soon she realizes it's the sound of horses galloping. After a little while, Emma hears voices.

"What's down there?" a man asks from above.

"That is a well that hasn't been used for years," a voice answers. Emma remembers the voice. It is the old man from the night before.

"Samuel, move that cover so we can have a look."

Emma holds her breath as the voices get louder.

Suddenly, dogs start barking in the distance.

"The hounds have picked up a scent in the woods," says another man.

"All right. We'll go have a look in the woods. But if those slaves turn up near your house, old man, you will have a lot of explaining to do!"

In the well, Emma lets out her breath. They are safe from the **slave trackers**—for now.

That night, the old man comes to help them out of the well. They say goodbye to him and start to run. As the sun rises, they come to a farm. They spend the day hiding in a haystack.

Days and nights go on like this. Each day they hide, and each night they run to another station on the Underground Railroad. Sometimes the conductor is a man and sometimes it is a woman or a young girl.

One night Papa Roland stops suddenly in front of a carved stone that is sticking out of the ground.

"Roland, are you sick?"
asks Sister-Ann.

"No, I'm not sick," replies
Papa Roland. "We just crossed the
Mason-Dixon line!"

"The border between Maryland
and Pennsylvania," Emma says.
"We're in the North!"

They all laugh and dance for
joy. But Papa Roland quiets them.

"We can't stop running until
we are in Canada," he says.

Chapter 5

The Welcoming

They travel through deep woods and over mountains. Secret signs along the way tell them where to go. Soon they see a farm up ahead. Emma hopes it is their next station. Suddenly, the door of the farmhouse swings open. A smiling black couple steps out.

The couple greets them. "Welcome! Come in!"

Emma looks at Sister-Ann. "We're going into their house?" she asks.

Sister-Ann smiles and nods. In all their travels, they have never been asked into someone's home.

Emma feels safe for the first time since this all began.

"I'm Edwina and this is my husband, Daniel," says the woman. She hands Emma and the others clean clothes and leads them to a trapdoor in the floor. They climb down narrow stairs and into a big, clean room where there are tables, chairs and beds.

Emma sits on one of the beds and sniffs the good smell of clean sheets and clothes. The twins watch her. They giggle and sniff the sheets and clothes, too.

Sister-Ann and Edwina pull out a large tub and fill it with warm water from teakettles. The twins and Emma take turns bathing. Then Emma crawls into a bed with the twins. As soon as her head hits the pillow, she falls sound asleep.

The others talk and make plans. Edwina tells them that she has always been free. Her parents left her the farm.

"Daniel showed up on the farm one night. He told me he was a runaway slave. He looked so brave and strong that I fell in love with him right then! We've been helping runaway slaves ever since."

Chapter 6

Freedom at Last

Emma and the others spend their days in the large room. They only leave the room at night.

After a few days, Papa Roland announces that it is time to go. Their journey is almost over.

They leave the house late at night and run and run. They are almost in Canada.

Close to daylight, Papa Roland stops running. "Get down!" he shouts. They all drop onto their stomachs and stay still for a long time. It gets very hot and Emma lifts her head to wipe her face.

"Keep your head down, Emma," Papa Roland whispers.

After a long time, it finally begins to grow dark.

"You can sit up now, honey," whispers Sister-Ann.

Emma sits up stiffly and yawns.

"Where is Papa Roland?" Emma asks.

"He is with Ben-John. They are waiting for us at the river. Here, have something to eat."

Emma and the twins quickly eat some food that Sister-Ann gives them. Then they follow Sister-Ann to the river.

When they reach the river, Papa Roland helps them into a rowboat. The boat rocks back and forth and the water splashes against its sides.

Emma closes her tired eyes.

"Emma! Emma! Wake up! You're free!" Sister-Ann shouts at the top of her lungs. Emma sits up and rubs her eyes.

Free? Emma has never heard a more wonderful word in all her life.

"My baby, my baby!" A woman runs to Emma. Tears of joy run down her face. It is her mother. Papa Roland wraps his arms around both of them.

"My family is together again. Together and free!" Papa Roland shouts.

Everyone is laughing and hugging and dancing. Emma twirls around and around until she is too dizzy to stand. She falls down in the grass.

"Why were you twirling around like that, Emma?" asks Tomas.

Emma looks around. Everything seems bright and clear and—free!

"Where were you? We've been looking everywhere!" Kevin says.

"Oh, I stopped to draw some pretty flowers," Emma tells them. "Did I miss much?"

"Well, there was a trail through the woods, just like the runaways used on the Underground Railroad," says Lucy. "I'll take you there if you want to see it."

"No thanks," says Emma, smiling. "I think I've seen enough trails for now!"

Glossary

Conductor: an individual who risked his or her life to take slaves from station to station on the Underground Railroad.

Mason-Dixon line: the border between Maryland and Pennsylvania, which became the dividing line between the slave-owning South and the North, where most people did not own slaves.

Slave trackers: People who followed and tried to catch runaway slaves, often using bloodhounds, with the hope of getting reward money.

Underground Railroad: a network of people and places set up to help slaves escape to freedom between 1830 and 1865. This network extended from the South to the northern part of the United States and into Canada.

About the Underground Railroad

The Underground Railroad was not a real railroad. It was made up of paths, stops and landmarks that began in the South, ran through the North and ended in Canada. The border between Maryland and Pennsylvania was called the Mason-Dixon line. It separated the slave-owning states of the South from the North. Most people in the North did not own slaves. Between 1830 and 1865, it is believed that about one hundred thousand slaves traveled the Underground Railroad.

Runaways on the Underground Railroad usually traveled at night. They followed the North Star, and relied on the "railways" of secretly marked paths, back roads, fields and tunnels. They also traveled on rivers, streams and other waterways, because no footprints were left behind. During the day, runaways hid in safe "stations," such as barn lofts and secret rooms in houses and churches.

Free people, both black and white,
who helped slaves escape were known
as "conductors" or "stationmasters."

Even though the Underground Railroad was a secret operation, its story was kept alive after slavery ended in1865. The Underground Railroad will always be remembered as a movement that worked to stop the mistreatment of human beings.